Lance Dragon Defends His Castle with SIMPLE MACHINES

by **Eric Braun**

illustrated by **Anthony Briglia**

PICTURE WINDOW BOOKS
a capstone imprint

Thanks to our advisers for their expertise, research, and advice:
Dr. Paul Ohmann, Associate Professor of Physics, University of St. Thomas
Terry Flaherty, PhD, Professor of English, Minnesota State University, Mankato

Editor: **Shelly Lyons**
Designer: **Lori Bye**
Art Director: **Nathan Gassman**
Production Specialist: **Danielle Ceminsky**
The illustrations in this book were created digitally.

Picture Window Books
1710 Roe Crest Drive
North Mankato, MN 56003
www.capstonepub.com

Library of Congress Cataloging-in-Publication Data
Braun, Eric, 1971-
Lance Dragon defends his castle with simple machines / by Eric Braun ;
illustrations by Anthony Briglia.
    p. cm. — (Picture Window Books. In the science lab)
 Includes bibliographical references and index.
ISBN 978-1-4048-7372-8 (library binding)
ISBN 978-1-4048-7708-5 (paperback)
ISBN 978-1-4048-7985-0 (ebook PDF)
1. Power (Mechanics)—Juvenile literature. I. Briglia, Anthony, ill.
II. Title.

 TJ163.95.B73 2013
 621.8—dc23

                    2012001009

Printed in the United States of America in North Mankato, Minnesota.
042012   006682CGF12

My name is **LANCE DRAGON**, and I don't like to fight.

I prefer to skate inside my castle. But I have no choice. Barbarians are at the gate! Luckily, I am one smart dragon (I'm sure you will agree). I know how to use simple machines to defend my castle.

3

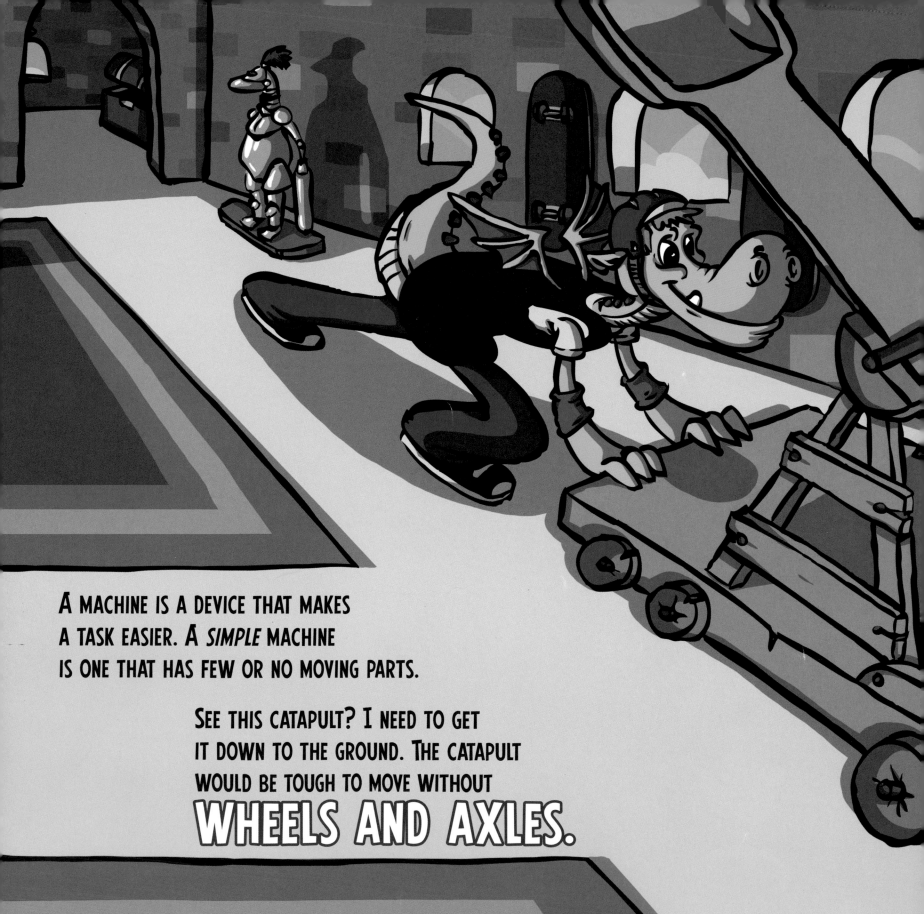

A MACHINE IS A DEVICE THAT MAKES
A TASK EASIER. A *SIMPLE* MACHINE
IS ONE THAT HAS FEW OR NO MOVING PARTS.

SEE THIS CATAPULT? I NEED TO GET
IT DOWN TO THE GROUND. THE CATAPULT
WOULD BE TOUGH TO MOVE WITHOUT
WHEELS AND AXLES.

A WHEEL AND AXLE IS A SIMPLE MACHINE.

An axle is a rod that goes through a large circle called a wheel. The axle allows the wheel to roll in place. Because a wheel is round, it doesn't take much force to turn it. The wheel and axle makes moving the catapult easier, because each of the wheels rolls.

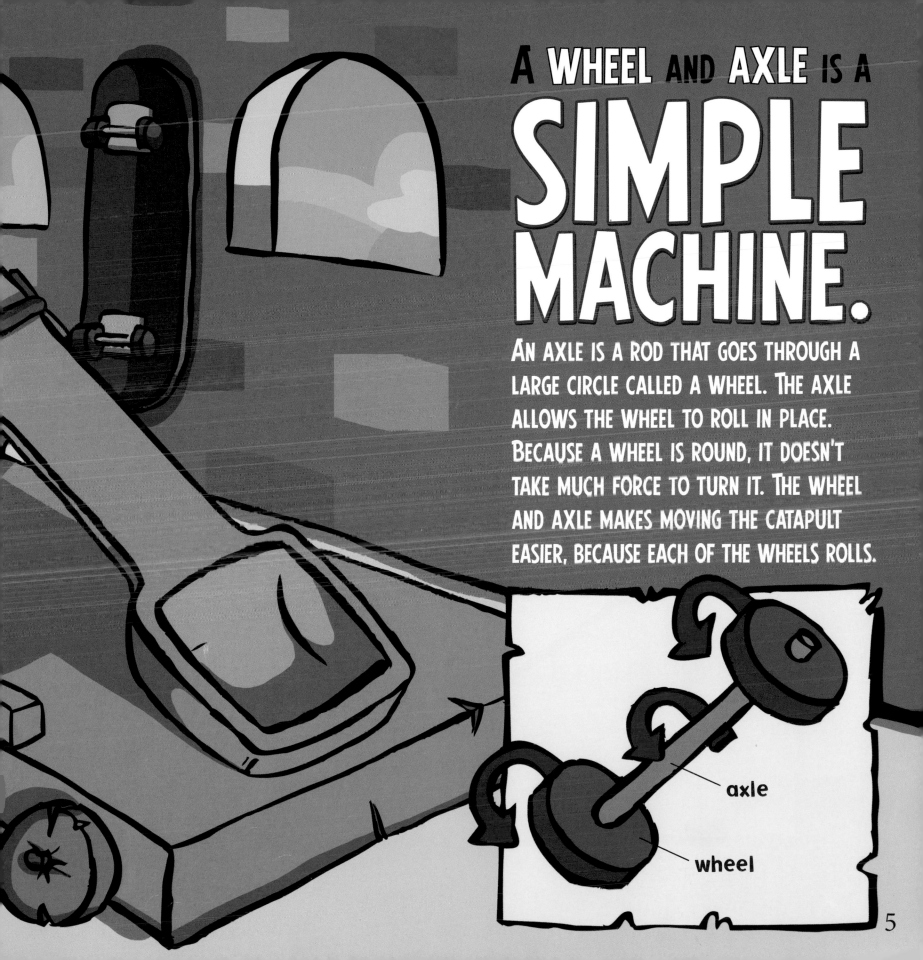

axle

wheel

5

EVEN WITH THE WHEEL AND AXLE, THE CATAPULT WOULD BE HARD TO MOVE DOWN A LEVEL WITHOUT A RAMP. THE RAMP IS A SIMPLE MACHINE CALLED AN **INCLINED PLANE.**
AN INCLINED PLANE IS A FLAT SURFACE THAT IS SLANTED. IT MAKES LIFTING OR LOWERING A LOAD EASIER.

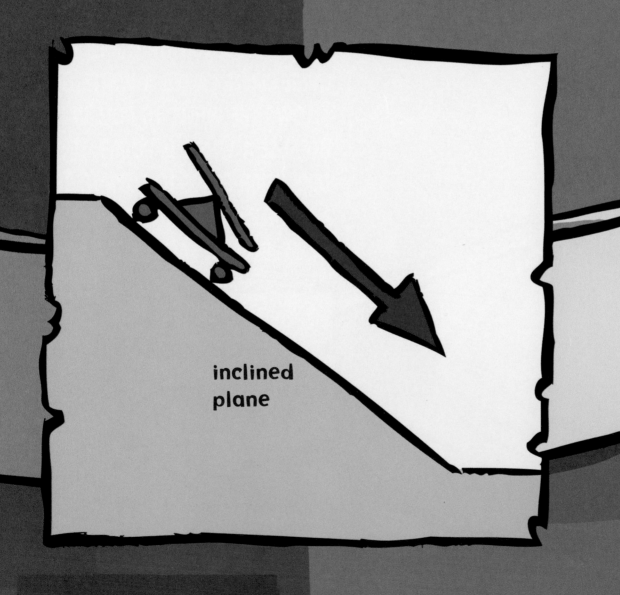

inclined
plane

A catapult is made from another simple machine called a **LEVER.**
A lever is a bar that rests on a point called a fulcrum.

8

The bar pivots on the fulcrum. When you move one end of the bar, the other end moves in the opposite direction. Watch what happens when I drop this rock on one end of the lever.

bar

fulcrum

Now I need to get upstairs. **STAIRS** are a simple machine. Like a ramp, they are an inclined plane, except each step is flat.

stairs

SIMPLE MACHINES ARE REALLY COMMON.

In fact, the lid on this jar is a simple machine called a **SCREW.**
A screw is a narrow inclined plane wrapped around something round.

ITCHING POWDER

screw

See how the groove, or plane, of the lid goes around and gets higher? When twisted onto the screw of the jar, the lid gets tight. When twisted in the other direction, the lid gets loose.

Behold as I unscrew this jar so I can surprise the barbarians. Ha, ha!

WELL, THIS IS EMBARRASSING. "WHY DIDN'T YOU SAY SO? HERE'S THE KEY."

I'll use this simple machine called a
PULLEY
to lower the key.

A pulley is a wheel and a rope. The wheel has a groove around the outside. The rope fits in the groove. A pulley makes it easier to move a load, like this heavy key.

pulley

I have one more simple machine to show you—my skateboarding ramp! It's an inclined plane, of course. But if a machine is something that makes a task easier, what task does this ramp make easier?

CATCHING AIR!

GLOSSARY

axle—a rod in the center of a wheel; usually it connects two wheels that turn around it

fulcrum—the point that a lever rests or turns on

inclined plane—a flat surface that is slanted so that things can be easily moved up and down along it

lever—a bar or board that pivots on a fulcrum; when one end is moved, the other end moves in the opposite direction to lift or move an object

pulley—a wheel, usually with a groove around the outside so that a rope or cable can fit into it; it is used to lift or lower loads more easily

screw—a narrow inclined plane wrapped around a cylinder so that when it is turned onto or Into something it tightens or loosens

simple machine—a machine with few or no moving parts

wedge—two inclined planes attached back to back so they create a sharp point that can be used to split things

wheel—a round frame or object that turns on an axle; when turned, the wheel moves a greater distance than the axle and takes less force to do so

TO LEARN MORE

More Books to Read

Salas, Laura Purdie. *Move It! Work It!: A Song About Simple Machines.* Science Songs. Minneapolis: Picture Window Books, 2009.

Silverman, Buffy. *I Use Simple Machines.* My Science Library. Vero Beach, Calif.: Rourke, Pub., 2010.

Weakland, Mark. *Gears Go, Wheels Roll.* Science Starts. Mankato, Minn.: Capstone Press, 2011.

Internet Sites

FactHound offers a safe, fun way to find Internet sites related to this book. All of the sites on FactHound have been researched by our staff.

Here's all you do:

Visit *www.facthound.com*

Type in this code: 9781404873728

Super-cool stuff! Check out projects, games and lots more at **www.capstonekids.com**

InDEx

LOOK FOR ALL THE BOOKS IN THE SERIES:

CAPTAIN KIDD'S CREW EXPERIMENTS WITH
SINKING AND FLOATING

DO-4U THE ROBOT EXPERIENCES
FORCES AND MOTION

Gertrude and Reginald the Monsters Talk about
LIVING AND NONLIVING

JOE-JOE THE WIZARD BREWS UP
SOLIDS, LIQUIDS, AND GASES

LANCE DRAGON DEFENDS HIS CASTLE WITH
SIMPLE MACHINES

MAD MARGARET EXPERIMENTS WITH THE
SCIENTIFIC METHOD

24